MODERN MASTERS OF SCIENCE FICTION

BY JOHN HAMILTON

Visit us at

www.abdopublishing.com

Published by ABDO Publishing Company, 4940 Viking Drive, Suite 622, Edina, Minnesota 55435.
Copyright ©2007 by Abdo Consulting Group, Inc. International copyrights reserved in all countries.
No part of this book may be reproduced in any form without written permission from the publisher.
ABDO & Daughters™ is a trademark and logo of ABDO Publishing Company.

Printed in the United States.

Editor: Paul Joseph
Graphic Design: John Hamilton
Cover Design: Neil Klinepier
Cover Illustration: Michael Crichton, Corbis
Interior Photos and Illustrations: p 1 astronaut and spaceship, Corbis; p 4 cover of *Ilium*, courtesy
Harper Collins; p 5 Dan Simmons, Corbis; p 6 scene from *Jurassic Park*, Corbis; p 7 Michael Crichton,
Corbis; p 8 *Neuromancer*, courtesy Ace Science Fiction; p 9 William Gibson, Corbis; p 10 cover of *Mars*,
courtesy Bantam Spectra; p 11 cover of *The Silent War*, courtesy Tom Doherty Associates; p 12 cover of
Gateway, courtesy Ballantine Books; p 13 *Demon in the Skull* ©1984 Don Maitz; p 14 cover of April
1974 issue, courtesy *Magazine of Fantasy and Science Fiction*; p 15 cover of *Roma Eterna*, courtesy Harper
Collins; p 16 cover of *Parable of the Talents*, courtesy Warner Books; p 17 Octavia Butler, courtesy Miami
Book Fair International; p 18 Kim Stanley Robinson, photo courtesy Szymon Sokol; p 19 cover of *Red
Mars*, courtesy Bantam Spectra; p 20 cover of *Neverwhere*, courtesy Harper Collins; p 21 Neil Gaiman,
Corbis; p 23 cover of *Dragonflight*, courtesy Ballantine Books; p 24 cover of *Kiln People*, courtesy Tom
Doherty Associates; p 25 portrait, courtesy David Brin; p 27 cover of *Speaker for the Dead*, courtesy Tom
Doherty Associates; p 28 *Pyramids of Technology*, Corbis; p 29 boy enters circuit board head, Corbis.

Library of Congress Cataloging-in-Publication Data

Hamilton, John, 1959-
    Modern masters of science fiction / John Hamilton.
    p. cm. -- (The world of science fiction)
    Includes index.
    ISBN-13: 978-1-59679-990-5
    ISBN-10: 1-59679-990-0
    1. Authors, American--20th century--Biography--Juvenile literature. 2. Science fiction, American--
History and criticism--Juvenile literature. 3. Science fiction--Authorship--Juvenile literature. I. Title.
II. Series: Hamilton, John, 1959- World of science fiction.

    PS129H363 2006
    823'.0876209--dc22
    [B]
    2006016392

CONTENTS

Dan Simmons 4

Michael Crichton 6

William Gibson 8

Ben Bova 10

Frederik Pohl 12

Robert Silverberg 14

Octavia Butler 16

Kim Stanley Robinson 18

Neil Gaiman 20

Anne McCaffrey 22

David Brin 24

Orson Scott Card 26

The Future of Science Fiction 28

Glossary 30

Index 32

DAN SIMMONS

The Hegemony Consul sat on the balcony of his ebony spaceship and played Rachmaninoff's Prelude in C-sharp Minor on an ancient but well-maintained Steinway while great, green, saurian things surged and bellowed in the swamps below.
—from *Hyperion*, by Dan Simmons

Dan Simmons writes some of the most exciting, thought-provoking, infuriating, stay-up-late, page-turning science fiction on the planet. But he won't tell you that. Simmons says he's merely honoring the great science fiction writers who came before him, celebrating their style with his own unique twist. His fans know better.

Dan Simmons writes outstanding mysteries, horror, and fantasy, but he's best known for his 1989 debut science fiction novel, *Hyperion*. This Hugo Award-winning novel is set in the far future, and tells the story of a group of pilgrims traveling across a strange planet on their way to a remote valley filled with mysterious Time Tombs. Simmons wrote three sequels: *The Fall of Hyperion*, *Endymion*, and *The Rise of Endymion*. Together, they are known as the *Hyperion Cantos*.

Facing page: Author Dan Simmons. *Below:* The cover of Dan Simmons' *Ilium*.

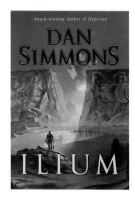

Dan Simmons was born in 1948, in Peoria, Illinois. He grew up in the Midwest. A former elementary school teacher, he sold his first short story, *The River Styx Runs Upstream*, in 1982. Today he lives and writes in Colorado, at the foothills of the Rocky Mountains.

Simmons masterfully weaves complex plots and themes into his novels, yet they are also spellbinding tales of adventure. The scientific details are utterly believable, but it is the human drama that is most memorable.

His most recent sci fi novels, *Ilium* and *Olympos*, fuse a wildly inventive plot with the legendary tale of Homer's *Iliad*. The story includes the Greek heroes Achilles and Odysseus, Olympian gods, and the war between Greece and Troy, all set in a far-future solar system with terrifying alien creatures, heroic robots, and a terraformed Mars. Simmons' writing is science fiction at its best.

MICHAEL CRICHTON

He saw the huge head of the tyrannosaurus. Just standing there, looking over the fence at the two Land Cruisers. The lightning flashed again, and the big animal rolled its head and bellowed in the glaring light. The darkness, and silence again, and the pounding rain.
—From *Jurassic Park*, by Michael Crichton

Michael Crichton isn't just an author—he's a one-man industry. Year after year, he cranks out best-selling novels, writes screenplays, and produces and directs award-winning TV shows and blockbuster films. He's like an unstoppable literary machine, and at 6-feet, 9-inches tall (206 cm), he literally stands a head above his peers. His books have sold more than 150 million copies in 36 languages. Thirteen have been made into movies.

Crichton was born on October 23, 1942, in Chicago, Illinois. He was raised on Long Island, New York, and earned an M.D. degree from Harvard Medical School. Crichton says on his website, "I wanted to become a writer but I didn't think it was likely I could make a living at it, so I went to medical school. … Then I started writing paperback thrillers to pay my way through medical school, and the books began to be successful. Finally I just decided to do it full time, after graduation."

Because he writes so many different kinds of fiction, he dislikes being called a science fiction author. Instead, he prefers to be called a writer of speculative fiction, or technological thrillers. Whatever one calls them, his tales are some of the most popular ever created. His sci fi blockbusters include: *The Andromeda Strain*, *The Terminal Man*, *Sphere*, *Jurassic Park*, *The Lost World*, *Timeline*, and *Prey*.

Facing page: Author Michael Crichton at work.
Below: A scene from *Jurassic Park*.

WILLIAM GIBSON

The sky above the port was the color of television, tuned to a dead channel.
—from *Neuromancer*, by William Gibson

William Gibson is often called the father of cyberpunk. Cyberpunk is a science fiction sub-category that usually takes place in a frightening, troubled future society. Common elements include Internet use (and abuse), mega-corporations, artificial intelligence (with machines that think like humans), and a society where the social order has broken down.

Gibson was born on March 17, 1948, in Conway, South Carolina. Today he lives and writes in Canada. Gibson's cyberpunk stories have a bleak style. They feature social commentary combined with high technology. *Neuromancer* was his first novel, published in 1984. It's the story of Charles Case, a brilliant "cyber-cowboy" who hacks into the digital world of cyberspace to help free an artificial intelligence. *Neuromancer* was a groundbreaking novel that explored many ideas about technology before they became popular, including virtual reality, artificial intelligence, and cyberspace.

Neuromancer was the first novel ever to win all three of the most important science fiction awards: the Hugo, the Nebula, and the Philip K. Dick Memorial Award. It continues in popularity, having sold more than 6.5 million copies to date. Some of Gibson's other works include *Mona Lisa Overdrive*, *Virtual Light*, and *Johnny Mnemonic*.

Interestingly, Gibson has never been overly fond of computers. He credits his success more to hard work and practice than a special skill with technology. On his personal website, Gibson writes, "I suspect I have spent just about exactly as much time actually writing as the average person my age has spent watching television, and that, as much as anything, may be the real secret here."

Facing page: William Gibson. *Below:* The cover of Gibson's groundbreaking novel, *Neuromancer*.

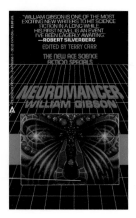

BEN BOVA

"Touchdown."

It was said in Russian first and then immediately repeated in English.

Jamie Waterman never felt the actual moment when they touched the surface of Mars. … Beyond everything else, Vosnesensky was a superb pilot.

—from *Mars,* by Ben Bova

Facing page: Ben Bova's *The Silent War.*
Below: The cover of Bova's epic novel, *Mars,* with art by Pamela Lee.

Early in his career, science fiction author Ben Bova had some big shoes to fill. In 1971, legendary writer and magazine editor John W. Campbell, Jr., died. He left his pioneering magazine, *Analog Science Fiction*, in the capable hands of Bova, who stayed at the helm for six years. Bova later became editorial director of *Omni*, helping discover and nurture new science fiction writers who would turn that magazine into a groundbreaking hit. Bova received the Hugo Award for Best Professional Editor six times.

Ben Bova was born November 8, 1932, in Philadelphia, Pennsylvania. He is the author of more than 100 books, both fiction and non-fiction. Bova is known for his "hard" science fiction books, which show how technology can be used to solve many of mankind's most difficult problems. His most recent novels together make up the *Ground Tour* series, which "combine romance, adventure, and the highest degree of scientific accuracy to show how the human race will expand through the solar system…" Some of the most popular books in this series include *The Silent War, Moonrise, Mars*, and *Saturn.*

BESTSELLING AUTHOR OF *DEATH DREAM* AND *BROTHERS*

BANTAM BOOKS

BEN BOVA
MARS

"A SWEEPING MICHENER-STYLE SAGA OF THE FIRST EXPEDITION TO OUR NEIGHBORING PLANET… THE ULTIMATE SUMMER ESCAPE." — *PEOPLE*

"Vintage Bova."
—*Booklist*

FREDERIK POHL

My name is Robinette Broadhead, in spite of which I am male. My analyst (whom I call Sigfrid von Shrink, although that isn't his name; he hasn't got a name, being a machine) has a lot of electronic fun with this fact…
—from *Gateway*, by Frederik Pohl

Facing page: Demon in the Skull, a portrait of Frederik Pohl by Don Maitz. *Below:* The cover of Frederik Pohl's *Gateway,* which won both the Hugo and Nebula Awards.

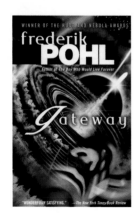

Frederik Pohl is considered one of the greatest science fiction writers still living and working today. Born on November 26, 1919, his science fiction career spans more than 60 years. He's been a writer, editor, fan, literary agent, critic, and even a struggling poet. He's won almost every award science fiction has to offer, including the Hugo Award (six times), the Nebula (three times), and the International John W. Campbell Award (twice).

Pohl is well known for creating mind-bending worlds, coupled with wit and humor. A former teacher and lecturer, Pohl enjoys offering social commentary as he entertains. One of his early novels, 1953's *The Space Merchants* (which he co-authored with Cyril M. Kornbluth) is a classic science fiction book about the importance of limiting population growth. It's a satire about an oppressive world run by advertising agencies. Pohl is the sole author of the sequel, *The Merchants' War,* written in 1984.

In 1977, Pohl published *Gateway,* which would be the first of several books that together make up the *Heechee* series. The Heechee are a star-traveling alien race who once explored Earth and the solar system thousands of years ago, but then mysteriously disappeared. In *Gateway,* humans discover abandoned Heechee spaceships. Brave explorers then proceed to take dangerous journeys throughout the galaxy in the alien ships. *Gateway* won the Hugo, Nebula, and John W. Campbell Awards for best novel.

Frederik Pohl doesn't seem to be slowing down anytime soon. In 2004, he published *The Boy Who Would Live Forever,* the next installment in the *Heechee* saga.

ROBERT SILVERBERG

The newly arrived ambassador from the Eastern Emperor was rather younger than Faustus had expected him to be: a smallish sort, finely built, quite handsome in what was almost a girlish kind of way, though obviously capable and sharp, a man who would bear close watching.

—from *Roma Eterna*, by Robert Silverberg

Robert Silverberg is one of the most prolific science fiction writers working today. In the 1950s, when he was just starting out, he wrote more than one million words *per year* for four years. His energy and never-ending ideas astound even the most seasoned science fiction fan. So far, he's won five Nebula Awards and three Hugo Awards, and he's still going strong. Isaac Asimov once said of him, "Where Silverberg goes today, the rest of science fiction will go tomorrow!"

Silverberg was born January 15, 1935, in Brooklyn, New York. As a boy he loved science fiction. In 1949, he started a fan magazine ("fanzine") called *Spaceship*. He started writing fiction while attending New York's Columbia University. In 1954, he sold his first piece of science fiction, a short story called *Gorgon Planet,* to *Nebula Science Fiction,* a British magazine. Silverberg's first novel, *Revolt on Alpha C*, was published in 1955. The next year, he was given a Hugo Award as Most Promising New Author.

For the next several years, Silverberg sold many short stories to magazines that specialized in science fiction. In the 1960s, he began to sell more books, including 70 nonfiction books for younger readers.

In the late 1960s and early 1970s, Silverberg published some of his most influential work, including *A Time of Changes*, *The Masks of Time*, and *Nightwings*, which won the Hugo Award in 1969 for Best Novella.

Below: The April 1974 edition of *The Magazine of Fantasy and Science Fiction* was a special edition featuring author Robert Silverberg, with artwork by Ed Emshwiller.

After a brief "retirement" in the late 1970s, Silverberg returned to science fiction. His work is as strong as ever. In 1980, he published *Lord Valentine's Castle.* It was the first of a group of books called the *Majipoor* series, which mixed science fiction with fantasy, all set on a planet in which immigrant humans coexist with shape-changing native aliens. His most recent book, 2003's *Roma Eterna*, is an alternate history novel about a modern-day Roman Empire.

In 2004, Robert Silverberg was named a Grand Master by the Science Fiction Writers of America.

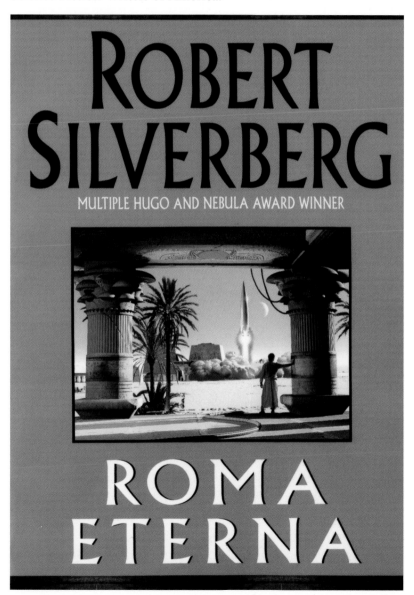

Left: The cover of Silverberg's *Roma Eterna.*

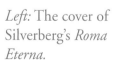

OCTAVIA BUTLER

I heard him move toward me, saw a blur of gray pants and blue shirt. Then, just before he would have touched me, he vanished.

The house, the books, everything vanished. Suddenly, I was outdoors kneeling on the ground beneath trees. I was in a green place. I was at the edge of a woods. Before me was a wide tranquil river, and near the middle of that river was a child splashing, screaming…

Drowning!

—from Kindred, *by Octavia Butler*

Octavia Butler was a Hugo and Nebula Award-winning author best known for her books about individuals who fight against injustice, and what it means to be part of a community. She was one of the very few African-American women to write professionally in the science fiction field. In 1995, she was the first science fiction author to ever receive a MacArthur Foundation "genius" grant, an award presented to American citizens who "show exceptional merit and promise for continued and enhanced creative work." She's best known for her powerful, passionate writing about themes of social justice.

Octavia Butler was born on June 22, 1947, in Pasadena, California. She grew up in Southern California in a poor neighborhood. Her father died when she was a baby, and her mother worked as a maid. She started writing at the age of 10 to escape loneliness. Early on, Butler was interested in reading science fiction magazines. Then, at age 12, she decided to try writing science fiction of her own. In an interview in *Black Scholar* magazine, Butler said, "… when I was 12, I was watching a bad science fiction movie, and decided that I could write a better story than that. And I turned off the TV and proceeded to try, and I've been writing science fiction ever since."

Butler's most famous novel was *Kindred*, published in 1979. It's the story of Dana, an African-American woman from 1976 who time-travels to the South in the days of slavery before the

Below: The cover of Octavia Butler's Nebula Award-winning novel, *Parable of the Talents.*

Civil War. Today it is required reading in many public schools and colleges.

Butler led a very successful and well-respected career for more than 30 years. She eventually moved to Seattle, Washington, in 1999. Tragically, her giant talent was cut short. She died after a fall at her home in February 2006. She'll be remembered for her hard work, her imagination and wit, and her passion for justice and understanding.

Below: A portrait of Octavia Butler.

KIM STANLEY ROBINSON

One day the sky fell. Plates of ice crashed into the lake, and then started thumping on the beach. The children scattered like frightened sandpipers. Nirgal ran over the dunes to the village and burst into the greenhouse, shouting, "The sky is falling, the sky is falling!" Peter sprinted out the doors and across the dunes faster than Nirgal could follow.

—from *Green Mars*, by Kim Stanley Robinson

Terraforming is the man-made process of making a planet livable for human beings. Of all the planets in our solar system, Mars is the most likely candidate for terraforming. The frozen, dead planet has been the subject of many stories about planetary engineering. The most popular is an epic series of three books (a *trilogy*) by science fiction writer Kim Stanley Robinson. His novels, *Red Mars* (1992), *Green Mars* (1993), and *Blue Mars* (1996), chronicle the human colonizing and terraforming of Earth's neighbor.

Facing page: Red Mars, the first part in Kim Stanley Robinson's popular *Mars* series.
Below: Kim Stanley Robinson.

Kim Stanley Robinson was born on March 23, 1952, in Waukegan, Illinois. He went to college at the University of California, San Diego, and Boston University. His fiction has won multiple Hugo and Nebula Awards. His books often explore themes of ecology and social justice. Robinson loves to mountain climb, which often shows up in his novels. His books, especially his *Mars* trilogy, are extremely popular by both fans and critics alike. He has a very sophisticated, literary style, with strong characterizations, which isn't often seen in science fiction.

Besides the *Mars* trilogy, Robinson is also famous for *Antarctica*, about scientists working in a cold, hostile environment, and *The Years of Rice and Salt*, an alternate history novel in which the Black Plague has wiped out the population of most of Europe, allowing Asian people to expand into the rest of the world.

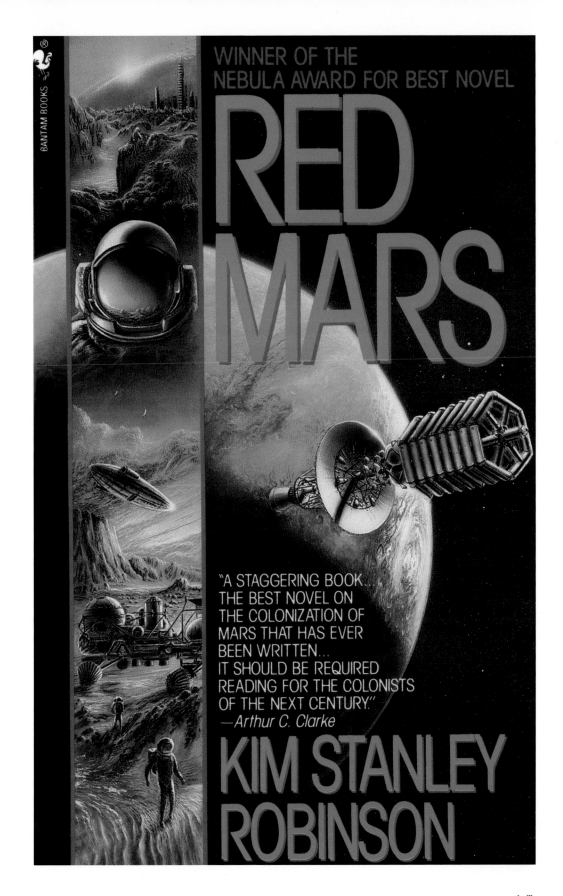

WINNER OF THE
NEBULA AWARD FOR BEST NOVEL

RED
MARS

"A STAGGERING BOOK...
THE BEST NOVEL ON
THE COLONIZATION OF
MARS THAT HAS EVER
BEEN WRITTEN...
IT SHOULD BE REQUIRED
READING FOR THE COLONISTS
OF THE NEXT CENTURY."
—*Arthur C. Clarke*

KIM STANLEY ROBINSON

NEIL GAIMAN

It begins, as most things begin, with a song.

In the beginning, after all, were the words, and they came with a tune. That was how the world was made, how the void was divided, how the lands and the stars and the dreams and the little gods and the animals, how all of them came into the world.

They were sung.

—from *Anansi Boys,* by Neil Gaiman

The Dictionary of Literary Biography lists fantasy and science fiction author Neil Gaiman as one of the top writers living and working today. His range of creativity is breathtaking: novels, short stories, comic books, journalism, song lyrics, drama, and screenplays.

Gaiman was born on November 10, 1960, in England, where he grew up. Today he lives and works in the United States, near Minneapolis, Minnesota. He started his career as a journalist, believing that it would help him learn about the world. His most popular early fiction was the *Sandman* series of comic books, published by DC Comics for 75 issues.

Gaiman's imaginative writing has netted him three Hugo Awards, two Nebula Awards, plus many other honors. He wrote his first children's book, *The Day I Swapped My Dad for Two Goldfish,* in 1997. *Newsweek* named it one of the best children's books of the year.

His recent Hugo Award-winning works include *Coraline, American Gods,* and *A Study in Emerald.* In 2005, he published *Anansi Boys,* which debuted on the *New York Times* bestsellers list. Like much of Gaiman's work, *Anansi Boys* is difficult to categorize. As Gaiman explains on his popular website, "It's a scary, funny sort of a story, which isn't exactly a thriller, and isn't really horror, and doesn't quite qualify as a ghost story (although it has at least one ghost in it), or a romantic comedy (although there are several romances in there, and it's certainly a comedy, except for the scary bits)."

Facing page: Neil Gaiman.
Below: The cover of Neil Gaiman's *Neverwhere.*

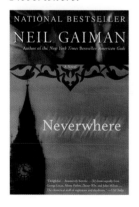

ANNE MCCAFFREY

These dragons—named for the mythical Terran beast they resembled—had two valuable characteristics: they could get from one place to another instantaneously and, after chewing a phosphine-bearing rock, they would emit a flaming gas. Because the dragons could fly, they were able to char Thread in midair, and then escape from its ravages.
—from *The White Dragon*, by Anne McCaffrey

Are dragons for real? Could they exist on Earth, or any other planet? They can indeed, at least in the vivid imagination of Anne McCaffrey, the American science fiction author best known for her *Dragonriders of Pern* series of books.

Anne Inez McCaffrey was born on April 1, 1926, in Cambridge, Massachusetts. She was educated in New Jersey and Virginia, and graduated with honors from Radcliffe College, Cambridge, majoring in literature and Slavic languages. She married in 1950 and had three children. After divorcing her husband in 1970, she moved to Ireland, where she still lives today, in a home she calls Dragonhold-Underhill.

By the time her children were old enough to go to school, McCaffrey had sold enough short stories to give her confidence to try writing novels full time. Her first novel was called *Restoree*, which was published in 1967. As her website states, *Restoree* "was written as a protest against the absurd and unrealistic portrayals of women in s-f novels in the 50s and early 60s."

Despite this early success, McCaffrey struggled as a novelist. She finally found success in 1978 when *The White Dragon* reached the *New York Times* bestsellers list, the first science fiction hardcover book ever to do so.

Of all her books, McCaffrey's *Pern* series is the most beloved by fans. Spanning 18 novels or novellas, plus several short stories, the series is about a planet named Pern, which is besieged every 200 years by destructive spores called Thread, which rain down from space. Specially bred creatures, which resemble dragons of Earth mythology, and their telepathically linked riders, are trained to fly into the air and destroy the Thread before it can reach the surface of Pern.

McCaffrey has won many awards for her imaginative work, including several Hugo and Nebula Awards. Today, from her home in Ireland, she still writes, collaborating with her son Todd, and continuing the Pern saga.

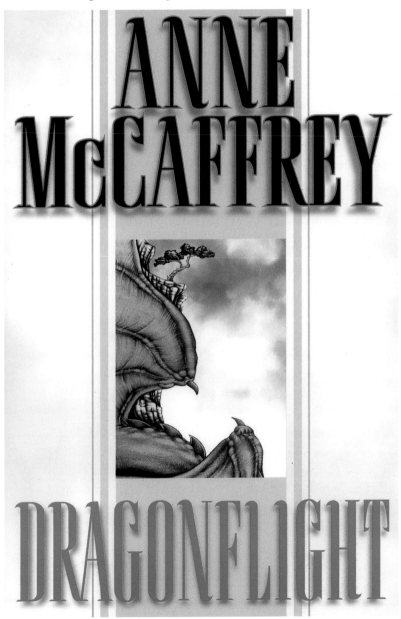

Left: Anne McCaffrey's *Dragonflight*, the first book in her *Dragonriders of Pern* series.

DAVID BRIN

It's hard to stay cordial while fighting for your life, even when your life doesn't amount to much.
Even when you're just a lump of clay.
—from *Kiln People*, by David Brin

David Brin takes care to tell people he is a scientist, first and foremost, not a *mere* science fiction author. He considers science to be a higher calling, a more worthy use of human effort. Yet, he recognizes that his main talent is to entertain, and so he writes his tales of science fiction, to the benefit of his grateful fans.

Glen David Brin was born on October 6, 1950, in Glendale, California. He has college degrees in astronomy, applied physics, and philosophy. His novels have appeared on the *New York Times* bestsellers list, and have won several Hugo and Nebula Awards, plus other awards as well.

In 1989, Brin wrote *Earth*, an ecological thriller that was nominated for a Hugo Award. The plot is about a manufactured black hole that is lost in Earth's interior, and the attempt to retrieve it before it destroys the planet. The book discuses several ecological problems we face today, such as global warming and ecoterrorism.

Brin's *Uplift* series includes six novels that tell of a galactic civilization that nurtures, or "uplifts," intelligent life in the galaxy. The third book in the series, *The Uplift War*, won the prestigious Hugo Award in 1988.

One of Brin's most recent novels is 2002's *Kiln People*. It's an inventive science fiction book written like an old-fashioned detective story. The novel is set in a future where people can make inexpensive clay copies of themselves to carry out boring or unpleasant day-to-day tasks. These "dittos" live for just a single day. Afterwards, their memories are uploaded into their creator's brain. It's an interesting and at times humorous story that mixes hard science fiction with questions of identity and privacy.

Facing page: Author David Brin.
Below: David Brin's 2002 novel, *Kiln People*, with cover art by Jim Burns.

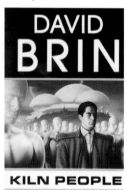

ORSON SCOTT CARD

Now Han Tsu remembered. Those last weeks in Command School—on Eros, when they thought they were in training but were really leading far-off fleets in the endgame of the war against the Hive Queens.
—from *Shadow of the Giant,* by Orson Scott Card

Orson Scott Card isn't afraid to share his secrets. The best-selling author of *Ender's Game* and *Speaker for the Dead* also conducts creative-writing workshops, has taught writing at several universities, and is the author of the popular book, *How to Write Science Fiction & Fantasy*. His personal website, "Hatrack River" (www.hatrack.com), also offers free lessons and advice for budding writers.

Orson Scott Card was born on August 24, 1951, in Richland, Washington. He grew up in Utah, California, and Arizona. He could often be found riding his bike to local libraries to read as many science fiction books as he could get his hands on. He also enjoyed classical literature, which would serve him well during his future writing career.

During his prolific career, Card has written dozens of novels, short stories, and stage plays. His science fiction is some of the most popular in the genre. His breakthrough novel was 1985's *Ender's Game*, about an invasion by insect-like aliens, and mankind's attempt to repel the invasion by breeding and training military geniuses at a young age. *Ender's Game* and its sequel, *Speaker for the Dead*, won back-to-back Hugo and Nebula Awards in 1985 and 1986.

Card's writing is filled with interesting characters who wrestle with moral issues. Card explains, "We care about moral issues, nobility, decency, happiness, goodness—the issues that matter in the real world, but which can only be addressed, in their purity, in fiction."

Facing page: The cover of Orson Scott Card's *Speaker for the Dead,* which won both the Hugo and Nebula Awards.

THE FUTURE OF SCIENCE FICTION

Has the future caught up with science fiction? Some people say that science fiction isn't as important as it once was because we're *already* living in the future. Computers, robots, satellites, space travel—this kind of "wild Buck Rogers stuff" is so common today that we take it all for granted. Science fiction writers continue speculating about the impact of technology on our society, but for the most part they've left stories of rocketships and time travel behind, focusing instead on more complex themes and issues.

In an interview with *Locus* magazine, author Robert Silverberg said, "People will go on writing good science fiction as long as there are ideas they want to play with. I don't think it's dead, but the struggle to fight the good fight gets harder and harder all the time."

Of course, there are still plenty of things for science fiction authors to write about in today's world: genetic engineering, advances in psychology, theoretical physics, computers that come closer and closer to mimicking life. Luckily for science fiction writers, and readers, our world has become a rapidly changing laboratory.

In a 1997 interview with CNN, William Gibson, author of *Neuromancer*, said, "…I felt that I was trying to describe an unthinkable present and I actually feel that science fiction's best use today is the exploration of contemporary reality rather than any attempt to predict where we are going… The best thing you can do with science today is use it to explore the present. Earth is the alien planet now."

Facing page: A boy enters a circuit board head, art by Joe Baker.
Below: Pyramids of Technology, by William Schick.

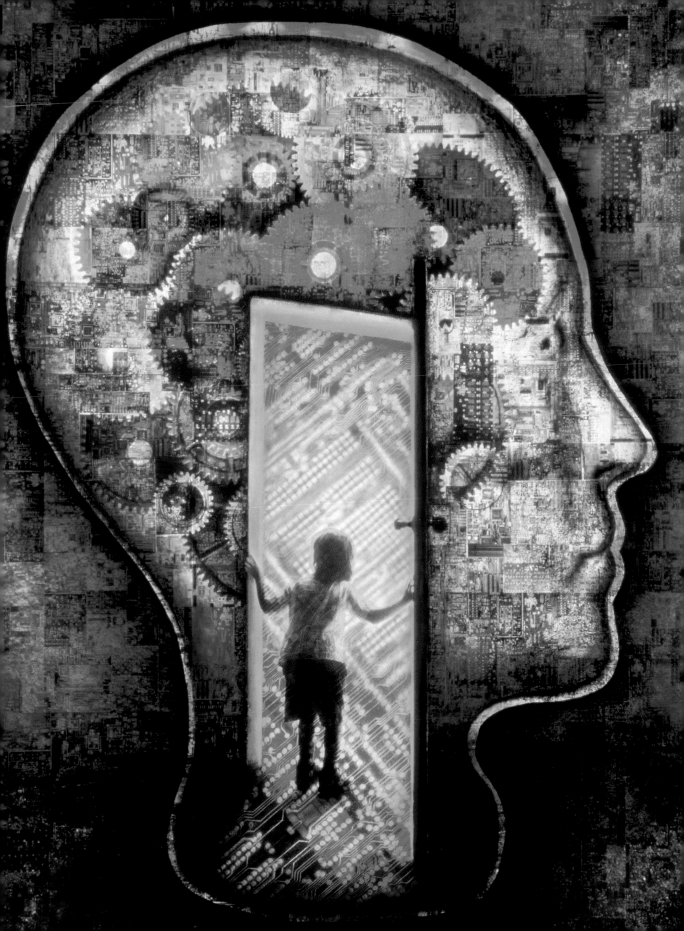

GLOSSARY

ARTIFICIAL INTELLIGENCE
A computer that is so advanced that it mimics human thought. Also referred to as AI.

CYBERPUNK
The word cyberpunk is a combination of the words punk and cybernetics, which is the science of control and communication of both machines and living creatures. Originally, it was meant to describe antisocial rebels who use computers to commit their crimes. Nowadays, cyberpunk more commonly refers to a tech-savvy hero who fights back, using the system against itself.

CYBERSPACE
A "virtual" reality that exists only inside the interconnected networks of advanced computers. The Internet is often called cyberspace.

GALAXY
A system of millions, or even hundreds of billions, of stars and planets, clustered together in a distinct shape, like a spiral or ellipse. Our Earth is located within the Milky Way Galaxy.

GENRE
A type, or kind, of a work of art. In literature, a genre is distinguished by a common subject, theme, or style. Some genres include science fiction, fantasy, and mystery.

HACKER
A criminal who illegally breaks into computer networks in order to steal information, or destroy and alter data files.

HUGO
The annual award presented by the World Science Fiction Society to honor the year's best science fiction. Named after the legendary writer and editor Hugo Gernsback, who founded *Amazing Stories* (left) in 1926.

NEBULA AWARDS
The prestigious annual award presented by the Science Fiction Writers of America (SFWA) for excellence in science fiction writing.

SATIRE
Using humor or exaggeration to point out and criticize people's stupidity. Satire is often used to criticize politics, but it is also used in literature such as science fiction.

SOLAR SYSTEM
The collection of planets, asteroids, and comets that orbit the sun. The solar system includes nine recognized planets: Mercury, Venus, Earth, Mars, Jupiter, Saturn, Uranus, Neptune, and Pluto.

SPECULATION
To guess, or form a theory, about what will happen, without firm evidence. Science fiction is often called speculative fiction, because its authors are making guesses about the future, usually based on trends they see happening today.

TERRAFORM
To make an alien planet more like Earth. In science fiction, terraforming is usually achieved with high technology, such as by "seeding" clouds with special chemicals to make them produce oxygen, so that future colonists can live on the planet.

TERRORISM
Using force and fear to weaken an opponent, such as by killing innocent civilians to make a political statement. The 2001 attacks on the World Trade Center and the Pentagon were acts of terrorism.

INDEX

A

Achilles 4
American Gods 20
Analog Science Fiction 10
Anansi Boys 20
Andromeda Strain, The 6
Antarctica 18
Arizona 26
Asimov, Isaac 14

B

Black Scholar 16
Blue Mars 18
Boston University 18
Bova, Ben 10
Boy Who Would Live Forever, The 12
Brin, David 24
Broadhead, Robinette 12
Brooklyn, NY 14
Butler, Octavia 16, 17

C

California 26
Cambridge, MA 22
Campbell, John W. Jr. 10
Canada 8
Card, Orson Scott 26
Case, Charles 8
Chicago, IL 6
Civil War 17
CNN 28
Colorado 4
Columbia University 14
Conway, SC 8
Coraline 20
Crichton, Michael 6

D

Day I Swapped My Dad for Two Goldfish, The 20
DC Comics 20
Dictionary of Literary Biography, The 20
Dragonhold-Underhill 22
Dragonriders of Pern 22

E

Earth 12, 22, 23, 24
Earth 24
Ender's Game 26
Endymion 4
England 20
Europe 18

F

Fall of Hyperion, The 4
Faustus 14

G

Gaiman, Neil 20
Gateway 12
Gibson, William 8, 28
Glendale, CA 24
Gorgon Planet 14
Grand Tour 10

Greece 4
Green Mars 18

H

Harvard Medical School 6
Heechee 12
Homer 4
How to Write Science Fiction & Fantasy 26
Hugo Award 4, 8, 10, 12, 14, 16, 18, 20, 23, 24, 26
Hyperion 4
Hyperion Cantos 4

I

Iliad 4
Ilium 4
International John W. Campbell Award 12
Internet 8
Ireland 22, 23

J

Johnny Mnemonic 8
Jurassic Park 6

K

Kiln People 24
Kindred 16
Kornbluth, Cyril M. 12

L

Locus 28
Long Island, NY 6
Lord Valentine's Castle 15
Lost World, The 6

M

MacArthur Foundation 16
Majipoor 15
Mars 4, 18
Mars 10
Mars (trilogy) 18
Masks of Time, The 14
McCaffrey, Anne 22, 23
McCaffrey, Todd 23
Merchants' War, The 12
Minneapolis, MN 20
Mona Lisa Overdrive 8
Moonrise 10

N

Nebula Award 8, 12, 14, 16, 18, 20, 23, 24, 26
Nebula Science Fiction 14
Neuromancer 8, 28
New Jersey 22
New York, NY 14
New York Times 20, 22, 24
Newsweek 20
Nightwings 14

O

Odysseus 4

Olympos 4
Omni 10

P

Pasadena, CA 16
Peoria, IL 4
Pern 22, 23
Philadelphia, PA 10
Philip K. Dick Memorial Award 8
Pohl, Frederik 12
Prey 6

R

Rachmaninoff 4
Radcliffe College 22
Red Mars 18
Restoree 22
Revolt on Alpha C 14
Richland, WA 26
Rise of Endymion, The 4
River Styx Runs Upstream, The 4
Robinson, Kim Stanley 18
Rocky Mountains 4
Rogers, Buck 28
Roma Eterna 14, 15
Roman Empire 15

S

Sandman 20
Saturn 10
Science Fiction Writers of America 15
Seattle, WA 17
Shadow of the Giant 26
Silent War, The 10
Silverberg, Robert 14, 15, 28
Simmons, Dan 4
Space Merchants, The 12
Spaceship 14
Speaker for the Dead 26
Sphere 6
Study in Emerald, A 20

T

Terminal Man, The 6
Time of Changes, A 14
Time Tombs 4
Timeline 6
Troy 4

U

United States 20
University of California, San Diego 18
Uplift 24
Uplift War, The 24
Utah 26

V

Virginia 22
Virtual Light 8

W

Waterman, Jamie 10
Waukegan, IL 18
White Dragon, The 22

Y

Years of Rice and Salt 18